A GIFT OF
JAPANESE COOKING

日本の料理

MIFUNE TSUJI

A Gift of
JAPANESE
COOKING

WEATHERHILL
New York & Tokyo

First edition, 1995
Second printing, 1996

Published jointly by Weatherhill, Inc.
568 Broadway, Suite 705, New York, N.Y. 10012
and Silent Books, Ltd., 10 Market Street, Swavesey,
Cambridge CB4 5QG, England

Illustrations reproduced courtesy of the British Library
and the Fitzwilliam Museum, Cambridge.
Calligraphy by Harumi Kanada. Typesetting by
Textype Typesetters, Cambridge, England.

Library of Congress Cataloging-in-Publication Data
    Tsuji, Mifune.
    A gift of Japanese cooking / Mifune Tsuji
        p.   cm.
    ISBN 0-8348-0347-X
    1. Cookery, Japanese.   I. Title.
    TX724.5.J3T835   1995
    641.5952—dc20   95-30010
                                                            CIP

Introduction

日
本
の
料
理

By way of an apology, I am a violinist, not a chef. However, when I was first approached to write a book on Japanese cooking I didn't feel my qualifications were lacking because I had never thought to write *that* kind of cookbook. I wanted to write a Japanese cookbook for Westerners who were, apart from the evident difference that I'm Japanese, like myself. This is a book for working people who enjoy good food that is a little bit out of the ordinary but don't have the time to go searching for exotic, expensive ingredients.

Japanese cuisine has become more popular in Western countries during the past decade. I first came to Europe in 1975 invited by Alberto Lysy to play with the *Camerata Lysy* and since then have travelled extensively throughout most countries of Europe, with trips also to America, the Philippines and Canada. I have always been pleased that no matter where I have been (even a small city in the middle of Texas!) I have been able to find Japanese restaurants. Most were very good: I found sushi restaurants in New York (before they were fashionable) that were the best I have tried anywhere, including Japan, and very reasonably priced. My musician and artist friends especially love Japanese food and we will often go to Japanese restaurants while on tour and they rely on me to interpret menus and introduce them to new dishes.

Despite this popularity of the sophisticated cuisine found in restaurants, very few Westerners are familiar with a more ordinary, everyday Japanese cookery. Perhaps it is the perception that it is all raw fish, seaweed and unrecognisable squishy things. More likely it is that commercial Western food chains have not yet put Japanese food into easy to understand, ready cooked, microwavable packages.

When I told my musician friends that I might write a Japanese cookbook, they were enthusiastic and encouraged me to cater fo. Western people who might not know anything about

Japanese food apart from restaurants. I myself didn't start preparing food on my own until my late twenties. Rather than due to a luxurious lifestyle, the reason for this had more to do with my career: I started to play the violin when I was three, and my mother didn't allow me to touch knives or hot pots and pans because she was afraid that I might do myself an injury. Eventually circumstances dictated that I start to follow a more domestic lifestyle and I took up cooking—especially Japanese—with a passion.

The problems I faced then are the ones that I hope this book will solve for you: how to prepare basic, simple Japanese food with ingredients readily to hand and without requiring years of specialised training. The recipes are not the typical ones that you might find in a Japanese restaurant—Japanese people normally don't eat like that. Also, traditional Japanese meals are usually served with many beautiful utensils in meticulous arrangements. However, a family eating at home or even entertaining will not normally go to such lengths.

I dedicate this book to my mother, Yoshiko Tsuji. She is a fantastic cook and many of the recipes here have originated with her.

I dropped my chopsticks at the cuckoo's songs,
Which I had not let fall at thunderclaps
Muchō [1738–1809]

Basic Japanese Ingredients

日
本
の
料
理

These days it is quite easy to find Japanese food shops in a large city and there you will certainly find everything you need. For those who don't live close to a large city, there are some alternatives. Chinese or Thai food shops are perhaps easier to find even in small towns and there you will find most of the materials.

Rice

To make Japanese-style rice, it is best to use Japanese rice. But unless you live in a large city where you can find Japanese shops, it is difficult to get it. It is possible to find California rice in Chinese or Thai shops, and this is very similar to Japanese rice. Otherwise you can use pudding rice which can be found in any supermarket.

Shōyu (Soy Sauce)

Soy sauce is a fermentation from soybeans, wheat, salt and water. Use Japanese soy sauce if you can get it. If you can't get it, use other varieties sparingly. Chinese soy sauce is not really suitable for Japanese cooking as it is too sweet.

Sake

This is Japanese rice wine. Most wine shops now stock this. For cooking, you don't need to buy expensive *sake*, unless you would like to enjoy drinking it while you cook! For drinking, it is normally served warm. Fill a small earthenware decanter and place it in a pot of near boiling water for a few minutes. Serve in small earthenware cups. If you can't get *sake*, substitute dry white wine or dry vermouth.

Unlike most other varieties of alcoholic beverage, *sake* will go bad after about a year, so a sniff before you drink would be prudent!

Mirin

Mirin is a sweetened *sake* used only for cooking. This might be a difficult ingredient to get but you can use *sake* and with a little sugar added to substitute.

Ginger

We use ginger, either ground or the juice from the root, in most meals. You can find ginger in almost any vegetable shop or supermarket.

Miso

This is bean paste which has been mixed with rice malt and allowed to ferment somewhat. It might not be easy to find except in Japanese food shops but I have occasionally found it in Chinese or Thai food shops. There are two varieties: red and white. The recipes in this book use only the red *miso* (*aka-miso*).

Tōfu

Tōfu is bean curd made from white soybeans. You can find *tōfu* in most large supermarkets or health food stores.

Shiitake

This is a variety of mushroom native to Japan. It comes in dried form and has recently become available in large supermarkets. Other large, dried mushrooms can also be substituted. To prepare the dried *shiitake*, remove the stems and soak in warm water for about 30 minutes or until softened.

Dashi

Dashi is a basic fish stock made from dried skipjack, or from *kombu* (seaweed). Depending on the meal, you will use *dashi* from skipjack or from *kombu* or from both. Alternatively, you can use *dashi-no-moto* which is a powder like bouillon cube. You simply saturate the cube in water and boil. Nowadays many Japanese use this package instead of making their own *dashi*. If you can't get *dashi* at all, chicken broth or chicken cubes may be substituted.

Wasabi

This is a green coloured substance which is a little bit like horse radish. Use only small amounts of *wasabi* to mix with soy sauce to make a dip for raw fish (*sashimi*). It is very sharp, so don't use too much.

How beautiful the bandit's wife,
Who is baking chestnuts for him
Rogetsu [1873–1927]

How to Cook Rice

Rice prepared for Japanese cooking is quite different from other Oriental cuisine. Rather than being dry, Japanese rice is wet and sticky. This is not entirely because of the type of rice (see Basic Japanese Ingredients) but more to do with the manner in which it is cooked.

Allow approximately 3 oz (75 g) dry rice per person. (This is quite a lot, but Japanese like to eat rice!)

At least 1 hour before serving, wash the rice three or four times in cold water, completely draining the water each time then soak the rice, filling the pot with water with 1.1 to 1.2 times the amount of rice, for at least 20 minutes.

Cook the rice over a high heat until boiling in a covered saucepan. A few seconds after the water reaches boiling, take off the lid and let it boil for about 15 seconds (or when you see several 'holes' in the rice made by the boiling action from the bottom of the pan). Put back the lid, turn down the heat to low and simmer for 10 minutes. Turn up the heat to full for 10 seconds and then turn off the heat completely.

Let the rice sit for at least 10 minutes in the covered saucepan before serving.

Extra cooked rice can be kept and reheated by steaming for 5 minutes.

A pot of tomatoes collects
All the colours of the balcony
Seihō [1882–?]

Artist unknown

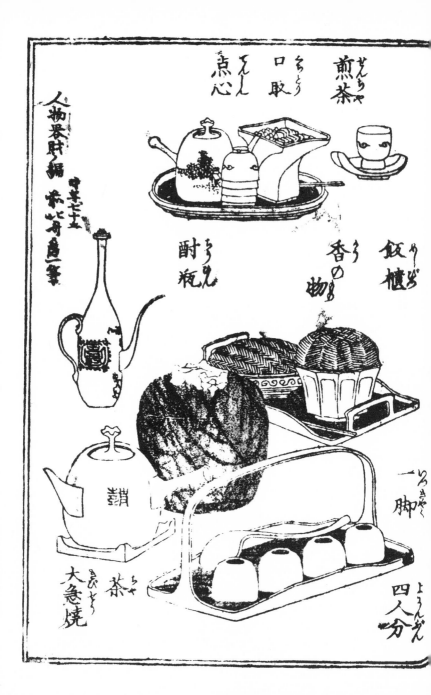

煎茶
せんちや

口取
くちとり

点心
てんしん

人物裏甲ノ編 茶ひ斗真一筆

酎瓶
ちろり

香の物
かうのもの

飯櫃
りうびつ

讃

一脚
いつきゃく

茶
ちや

大急焼
だいきうやき

四人分
よにんぶん

Hokusai

Recipes

日
本
の
料
理

Ah! I take my breakfast
Viewing morning glories
Bashō [1644–1694]

Kwaigetsudō Dohan

Hokusai

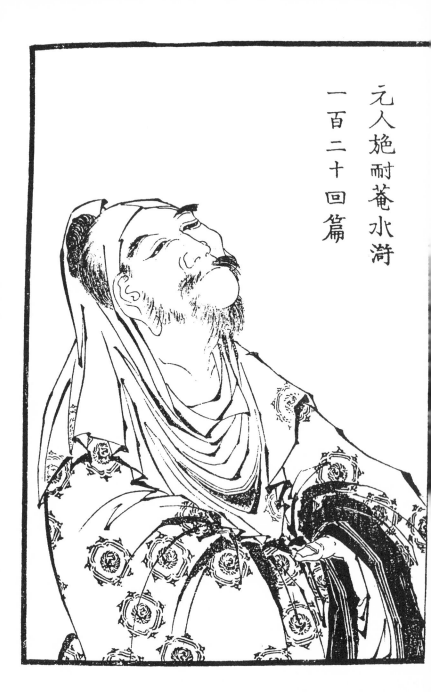

元人施耐菴水滸
一百二十回篇

Hokusai

Cooked Eggplant with Red Chilli Pepper

Serves 4

This is very simple but tasty, suitable as a summer dish. After cooking, place on a plate in the refrigerator, and eat cold.

3 eggplants (aubergines) (about 1 lb (500 g))
2 tsp salt dissolved in 2 pints (1.1 litres) water
1 red chilli pepper cut into small pieces
3 tbsp cooking oil
4 tsp sugar
3 tbsp soy sauce

Cut the eggplants in half and place in the salted water. Cover with a plate so that the pieces don't float. Remove and wipe off the water.

Heat the oil in a pan and cook the eggplant and red pepper for 5 minutes. Remove the pan from the heat and add water.

Return the pan to the heat and, when the mixture comes to the boil, add the sugar. Cook for 3~4 minutes on a medium heat. Add the soy sauce, turn over the vegetables a few times and cook until the liquid is reduced by a third.

What a bright harvest moon
My shadow walks home with me
Sodō [1641–1716]

Fried Tōfu and Pork

Serves 4

This is a delicious and filling main dish made with slices of pork over a bed of fried *tōfu*.

2 x 9 oz (285 g) packets of *tōfu*
10 oz (300 g) thinly sliced pork
Soy sauce
Sake
1 egg
½ tsp salt
5 tbsp flour
Salad oil
2 oz (50 g) cooked green peas
Pepper
4 fl oz (100 ml) water
2 tsp corn starch

Cut each *tōfu* into eight pieces and place on a kitchen paper to dry. Place the pork in a mixing bowl and add 1 tsp soy sauce and 1 tsp *sake*. Mix in well using your fingers.

Make a batter by mixing together the egg, salt, and flour. Cover the *tōfu* with the batter and fry in a small amount of salad oil over a medium head until the pieces are a golden colour on all sides. Remove the *tōfu* from the pan, set aside and keep warm.

Fry the pork, until it is well browned, then add the peas, 2 tbsp soy sauce, 2 tsp *sake*, and pepper. Mix together the water and corn starch. Add this to the liquid in the pan, stirring until it thickens.

Arrange the *tōfu* on a serving plate and pour the pork and sauce on top of them.

Kuwayaki (Chicken with Mushrooms)

Serves 4

This is chicken with a thick sauce and garnished with mushrooms.

10 oz (300 g) fillet of chicken breast
2 tbsp *sake*
1 oz (25 g) of flour
Salad oil
8 oyster mushrooms, cut in half
Prepare a mixture of: 3 tbsp *mirin* 5 tbsp soy sauce 3 tbsp *sake*

Cut the chicken into bite-sized pieces, sprinkle the *sake* evenly over them and work in well with your fingers. Coat the chicken with flour.

Heat some salad oil in a pan and quickly cook the mushrooms over a high heat. Set them aside. Add more salad oil to the pan and fry the chicken on both sides. Pour the *mirin* mixture evenly over the chicken. Add the mushrooms and cook together for 1 minute. Serve hot.

Serves 4

These hamburgers are very easy to prepare and are very popular in Japan.

10 oz (300 g) minced beef
1 egg
⅓ onion, minced
1 oz (25 g) breadcrumbs soaked in a little milk
½ tsp salt
1 tsp minced ginger
Flour
1 tbsp oil
1 tbsp butter
3 tbsp *sake*
2~3 tbsp sugar
4 tbsp soy sauce
4 tbsp water
Lettuce, to serve

Mix the beef, egg, onion, breadcrumbs, salt and ginger well by hand, divide into four and coat with flour. Heat the oil and butter together in a pan and cook the hamburgers over a high heat until brown. Turn over and cook for 6~7 minutes, covered, over a low heat.

Take out the hamburgers and discard the oil. Add to the pan the *sake*, sugar, soy sauce and water and bring to a boil.

22   Put the hamburgers back into the pan and cook for

5 minutes over a low~medium heat, pouring sauce over them occasionally.

For each serving, spread lettuce on a large plate to make a bed for the hamburger and pour over the remaining sauce.

Okra and White Radish

Serves 4

Japanese people love the stickiness of okra, and it makes a tasty side dish.

1 white radish
8 oz (250 g) okra
Soy sauce
Lemon juice
Cooked prawns, optional

Grate the white radish and squeeze out any excess water. Cook the okra in salted boiling water for 2 minutes then cut into small pieces and mix with the ground radish. Cool in the refrigerator for a while. Add soy sauce and lemon juice according to your own taste. Add the prawns if you wish. Serve in small bowls as a side dish.

How I envy the maple leafage
Which turns beautiful and then falls
Shikō [1664–1731]

常州江戸崎　綠樹園

永　七
七　十
六　夷
歳

上髙の
よみか
たの
窪さへよ八
や住らくありぬ
まちらめて
しく

Hokusai

Chicken Teriyaki

Serves 4

This is a dish of chicken breast fillets covered in a delicious sauce.

4 tbsp soy sauce
3 tbsp *sake*
2~3 tsp ginger juice
3 or 4 chicken breasts
3 tbsp salad oil
2 tbsp *mirin*
1 tbsp sugar

Mix together the soy sauce, *sake* and ginger juice in a medium bowl. Prick the skin of the chicken breasts with a fork and marinate them for 1 hour in the sauce. Turn the chicken over several times.

Heat the salad oil in a frying pan. Remove the chicken from the marinade and cook it skin side first. Turn it over, reduce the heat and cook for 10 minutes with a lid on.

Take out the chicken and drain the oil. Add the soy sauce marinade, the *mirin*, and the sugar to the pan and bring to a boil. Put the chicken back and cook for about 5 minutes over a medium~high heat to let the sauce thicken. Cover the chicken with the sauce.

To serve, slice the chicken into strips, pour the remaining sauce over them and place in a heated serving dish.

Pork Shōgayaki

Serves 4

Shōga is ginger. This is pork cooked in ginger sauce. It is one of the most popular dishes with the Japanese.

4 pieces of pork loin, about 5 oz (150 g) each

Prepare mixture A:
  3~4 tsp ginger juice
  1~2 tbsp *sake*
  1~2 tbsp *mirin*
  4 tbsp soy sauce

1 tbsp salad oil

Prepare mixture B:
  2 tbsp *mirin*
  1 tbsp sugar

Lettuce, to serve

Marinate the pork in mixture A for about 30 minutes, turning occasionally. Remove the meat from the marinade.

Preheat a large frying pan and add the salad oil. Fry the meat quickly squeezing out the liquid, until browned on both sides. Remove the meat from the pan and drain the oil.

Place both mixtures A and B in the pan and bring to the boil. Replace the meat and cook gently until the meat is tender (about 15 minutes). Occasionally spoon the liquid over the meat.

Tear the lettuce into small pieces and cover a plate. Place the meat on this and pour some of the sauce over. Lettuce with this juice is quite tasty.

Salmon Teriyaki

Serves 4

Teriyaki is cooked fish or chicken marinated with sauce. Instead of salmon, you can substitute tuna, Spanish mackerel or yellowtail.

4 medium pieces of salmon steak
Prepare mixture *A*: 3 tbsp soy sauce 2 tbsp *mirin*
2 tbsp salad oil
Prepare mixture B: 2 tbsp mirin ¼~1 tbsp sugar

Marinate the fish in mixture A for 1 hour, turning several times.

Preheat a large frying pan and add the salad oil. Fry the fish over a high heat for a few minutes on each side. Remove the fish from the pan and drain off the oil.

Bring mixtures *A* and *B* to a boil in the same pan, add the fish and cook over a medium heat until the juice thickens. Occasionally spoon the juice over the fish.

On cloudy days, all through the day,
The cherry-flowers shine on men
Kyohaku [?–1698]

Chicken and Potatoes Amakara Ni

Serves 4

This chicken and potato dish has a sweet, soy sauce flavour.

10 oz (300 g) chicken breast fillet
4 medium potatoes, peeled
2 carrots
1 medium onion, peeled
Salad oil
4 fl oz (100 ml) water
Prepare a mixture of: 1½ tbsp sugar 3 tbsp soy sauce 1½ tbsp sake
2 oz (50 g) snow peas

Cut the chicken, potatoes and carrots into bite sized pieces. Cut the onion into ¾ inch cubes.

Heat up the salad oil in a pan and cook the chicken, potatoes and carrots, stirring constantly. Add the water and the soy sauce mixture, and cook until all the liquid has been absorbed.

Cook the snow peas in salted boiling water for a few minutes, then drain them

Put chicken and vegetables on a bowl-like plate and scatter the snow peas on top.

Artist unknown

Artist unknown

Chawanmushi

Serves 4

This is a very charming supper custard.

Prepare a mixture of:
18 fl oz (500 ml) *dashi* (or chicken stock)
½ tsp salt
1 tsp *mirin*
1 tsp soy sauce

4 oz (125 g) chicken breast

Sake

4 oz (125 g) white fish

3 eggs, beaten

4 *shiitake* mushrooms

8 shrimps

A few watercress leaves

Prepare the *dashi* mixture and allow it to cool.

Cut the chicken into bite-sized pieces and coat with a little soy sauce and *sake*. Cut the white fish into bite-sized pieces and season with a pinch of salt and a little *sake*.

Mix the beaten eggs and cooled *dashi*, then put it through a strainer.

In each of four individual custard cups or casseroles place a *shiitake* mushroom, some chicken, and fish and pour the egg mixture on it. Put two shrimps and some watercress leaves on the top.

Put the custard cups in a steamer and steam for 2 minutes over high heat. Then reduce the heat and steam gently for 15 minutes or until the custard is set.

Chicken Liver with Bean Sprouts

Serves 4

This is a very typical and popular dish and is easy to prepare. It is usually served with rice.

14 oz (400 g) chicken livers
16 fl oz (450 ml) water
2 cloves garlic, crushed
4 tbsp salad oil
1 tbsp minced ginger
8 oz (250 g) bean sprouts
1 leek, washed and cut into bite-sized pieces
Prepare a mixture of: 1 tbsp *sake* ½ tsp salt 1 tbsp soy sauce Dash of pepper
1 tsp sesame oil

Cut the chicken livers into bite-sized pieces and soak in water for 30 minutes. Change the water a few times.

Boil the water with the garlic and boil the liver in this for a few seconds. Drain the water off.

Heat up a wok, heat 2 tbsp salad oil with the ginger and cook the liver until brown. Take out the liver. Add 2 tbsp salad oil and cook the bean sprouts and leek, put back the liver and season with the *sake* mixture. Sprinkle with sesame oil and serve over rice.

Squid Teriyaki

Serves 4

Do you like squid? Sometimes, depending on how it is cooked, squid can be difficult to chew. The way of preparing squid in this recipe is said to be for 'old people with weak teeth', because the squid becomes quite soft.

2 medium sized squid (body only)
2 tbsp *sake*
3 tbsp soy sauce
2 tbsp sugar
2 tsp corn starch
2 tbsp water

Gut the squid and rinse thoroughly. Cut into ½ inch (1 cm) slices.

Measure the *sake*, soy sauce and sugar into a pan and bring the mixture to the boil. Leaving it over a high heat, add the squid and stir with chopsticks quickly and continuously. Cook until the colour of the squid changes.

Remove the squid and continue to boil the liquid until it is reduced to one-third. Return the squid to the pan, cook for a few seconds and then remove again. Boil the sauce again to reduce it this time by one half.

Mix the corn starch and water in a small cup and add it to the sauce to thicken it. Again return the squid to the pan, and this time cook until the sauce is absorbed into the squid.

Serve hot with rice.

Satsuma Jiru

Serves 4

A simple Japanese countryside style soup with chicken and vegetables.

1 tbsp salad oil
4 chicken drumsticks or thighs
2 pints (1.1 litres) water
2 potatoes, peeled
2 carrots, peeled
6 tbsp *miso*
9 oz (285 g) packet of *tōfu*
1 leek

Heat the salad oil in a pan and fry the chicken. Add the water and bring this to a boil. Skim off the foam and lower the heat to a simmer.

Cut the potatoes and carrots into bite-sized pieces and add to the chicken. Return to a boil, skim off the foam and stir in 4 tbsp *miso*. Cook over a low heat for 20 minutes or until the vegetables are cooked.

Cut the *tōfu* and leek into bite sized pieces. Dissolve 2 tbsp *miso* in the soup and add the leeks and *tōfu*. Bring to the boil for only a few seconds. Remove from the heat and serve.

Yoshida Hanbei

Sukiyaki

This is perhaps the most popular and famous dish from Japan. It is prepared at the table with an electric or gas skillet. *Sukiyaki* is meat and vegetables cooked very quickly in a boiling broth, dipped in raw egg and eaten directly. If you are afraid of raw egg, you may leave it out, but that is the traditional way of serving and eating this dish.

3 leeks, washed

2 x 9 oz (285 g) packets of *tōfu*

¼ Chinese cabbage

2 lb 4 oz (1 kg) beef fillet sliced paper thin*

14 oz (400 g) can of bamboo shoots, drained

2 oz (50 g) sliced mushrooms

6 eggs

1 oz (25 g) beef suet (or 3 tbsp vegetable oil)

Prepare a mixture of:
   8 tbsp soy sauce
   3 tbsp *sake*
   3 tbsp *mirin*
   3 tbsp sugar

Hot rice

Cut the leeks diagonally into 1½ inch (4 cm) pieces. Cut the *tōfu* into 1¼ inch (3 cm) cubes. Cut the Chinese cabbage into bite-sized pieces. Arrange the sliced beef and vegetables beautifully on a large plate.

Prepare six bowls, one for each person, crack an egg into each of them and mix lightly.

In a hot, heavy pan melt the beef suet or oil, and fry one-third of the beef over a high heat for about 1 minute. Add the soy sauce mixture. When it boils add some of the vegetables and *tōfu* and keep at a medium heat. This will be ready in 1 or 2 minutes. Each person then takes the pieces out with chopsticks, dips them in the raw egg and eats them with rice.

As the ingredients are eaten, add the remaining meat and vegetables. If the sauce thickens, you may add a bit more soy sauce, *sake* and sugar, or add a little *dashi*.

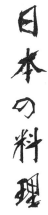

* The meat is easy to slice if you put it in the freezer for 40 minutes and use a very sharp knife. But when it is to be cooked, the meat should be at room temperature.

What a bright moon!
Mount Fuji is smaller than usual
Tōshi [?]

Chiri Nabe

Serves 4

This meal is cooked at the table like *sukiyaki.*

9 oz (285 g) packet of *tōfu*
16 oz (500 g) fresh spinach
12 *shiitake* or mushrooms
4 slices sea bream
3 leeks, washed
¼ Chinese cabbage
2½ pints (1.5 litres) water
Salt
Mix for a dip sauce: 4 tbsp lemon juice 2 fl oz (50 ml) soy sauce 4 tbsp grated white radish A dash of red pepper

Cut the *tōfu* into 1¼ inch (3 cm) cubes. Cut the spinach, cabbage and fish into bite sized pieces. Cut the leeks diagonally into 1½ inch (4 cm) pieces. Arrange the fish and vegetables attractively on a large plate.

Lightly salt the water and bring it to the boil in a large earthenware cooking pot together with the fish. Skim off the foam.

Add some of the cabbage, *shiitake*, leeks and *tōfu*. Cook briefly (2~3 minutes) add the spinach and cook for an additional minute. When everything is cooked, take out with chopsticks and place briefly in the dip before eating.

Mābo-Dōfu

Serves 4

Chinese in origin, *mābo-dōfu* has been adopted as a Japanese favourite. This is a hot, spicy *tōfu* and minced pork mixture.

---

2 x 9 oz (285 g) packets of *tōfu*

---

1 lb (500 g) minced pork

Prepare mixture A:
   1 tsp ginger juice
   2 tsp soy sauce
   2 tsp *sake*

---

3 tbsp salad oil

Prepare mixture B:
   1 red chilli pepper, minced
   ½ small leek, minced
   1 clove garlic, crushed
   1 chunk ginger (½ inch (1 cm) cube) minced

1½ tbsp *sake*

Prepare mixture C:
   3 tbsp miso
   1 tbsp sugar
   1/2 tsp salt
   1 beef bouillon cube
   8 fl oz (200 ml) water

---

1 tsp corn starch

---

2 tbsp water

Sesame oil

Cut the *tōfu* into ½ inch (1 cm) cubes. Add mixture A to the meat and blend well.

41

Heat up a wok, the salad oil and cook mixture B for about 15 seconds. Add the meat and cook over high heat until the meat is cooked. Pour the *sake* into the wok, not over the meat but down the side of the wok. Add mixture C and allow to come to a boil.

Add the *tōfu* and turn down the heat to medium. Mix and cook for 7 minutes, stirring occasionally.

Mix the corn starch with the water, add to the wok and stir gently to make the liquid thicker. Pour in a few drops of sesame oil, remove from the heat and serve over rice.

In the spring rain
All things grow beautiful
Chiyo-Ni [1701–1775]

Katsukawa Shunchō

小野川
髙嶌おひさ

Beef and Green Pepper Miso Itame

Serves 4

This means 'beef and green pepper cooked with miso taste'. A popular everyday meal.

14 oz (400 g) beef fillet thinly sliced (see *Sukiyaki*)

1 tbsp sake

2 tbsp soy sauce

½ leek, washed and minced

1 clove garlic, minced

4 tbsp salad oil

4 green peppers, deseeded and cut into lenthwise strips

Mix together:
   1 tbsp *miso*
   ½ tbsp soy sauce
   ½ tbsp *sake*
   1 tsp sugar
   Pinch of salt

Mix the sliced beef with the *sake*, and soy sauce and marinate for 10 minutes.

Heat the salad oil in a large wok and fry the minced leek and garlic for a few minutes. Add the beef and cook until brown. Add the green pepper and cook until soft, then add the *miso* mixture. Mix well and remove from the heat. Serve over rice.

Three-coloured Rice

Serves 4

This doesn't mean that the rice has three colours. On top of the rice, you cook and place three different things—beef mince, beans and eggs—thereby giving you three colours, brown, green and yellow.

10 oz (300 g) green beans
4 eggs
Pinch of salt
3 tbsp sugar
1 lb (500 g) beef mince

Mix together:
  5 tbsp soy sauce
  2 tbsp ginger juice
  4 tbsp *sake*
  2 tbsp sugar

Hot rice, to serve

Cook the beans in salted, boiling water for about 6 minutes. Remove and cut into bite-sized pieces.

In a medium pan, mix the eggs with a pinch of salt and the sugar. Heat up the pan, stirring constantly with two chopsticks. Occasionally lift the pan from the heat in order to avoid burning the eggs. Heat slowly like this until the eggs begin to resemble the texture of scrambled eggs. This is sweet egg, called *Iri-tamago,* and can be an easy side dish for many Japanese meals.

Blend the beef mince with the soy sauce mixture in another pan. Heat up the pan over a high heat and cook until the meat is brown and separated.

Serve over hot rice, making the beans, eggs and meat each into a triangle shape.

Mackerel with Miso

Serves 4

Japanese traditional folklore has it that in order to diminish the strong fish smell of mackerel one should always cook it with *miso* and ginger.

1 mackerel, approximately 1¼ ~1½ lb (625-750g) in weight

Mix together:
    3 fl oz (75 ml) *sake*
    8 fl oz (200 ml) water
    3 tbsp sugar
    1 tbsp soy sauce
    1½ inch (4 cm) piece of ginger root, sliced

2 green peppers

3 fl oz (75 ml) *mirin*

6 tbsp *miso*

3 fl oz (75 ml) *sake*

Remove the head, tail and bones from the mackerel and cut it into four pieces suitable for serving. Pour boiling water over the fish in order to take away some of the fish smell.

Put the *sake* mixture in a saucepan and bring to the boil. Add the fish and when it has reached boiling again reduce the heat and cook gently for 20 minutes.

Cut the green pepper lengthways into quarters. In a separate pan, boil them until soft.

Add the *mirin* and *miso* to the fish and continue boiling for 15 minutes over a medium heat. When the sauce thickens, add the *sake* and shake (don't stir) the pan to mix the contents.

Add the green pepper and cook for a few seconds. Put the fish and green pepper on a plate and cover them with the sauce.

46

Minced Chicken and Tōfu

Although the eating habits of most urban Japanese have been Westernised, older people and those from rural areas will still eat a Japanese style breakfast. Typically, this is hot rice, *nori* (seaweed), boiled fish, raw egg and *miso* soup, but occasionally they will add this dish to their breakfast.*

Salad oil
10 oz (300 g) minced chicken or turkey
Mix together: 8 fl oz (200 ml) *dashi* (or chicken stock) ½ tbsp ginger juice 2 tbsp soy sauce 2 tbsp sugar 1 tablespoon *sake* 1 tablespoon *mirin*
9 oz (285 g) packet of *tōfu*
Cooked snow peas, to garnish

In a heated pot, add a little salad oil and quickly braise the minced chicken or turkey. Add the *dashi* mixture.

Cut the *tōfu* into ¾ inch (2 cm) cubes and add to the chicken. Cook until the *tōfu* and chicken absorb the stock.

Place on a serving dish and garnish with the snow peas.

---

* Most Europeans would find this too heavy for breakfast but it makes a quick and nutritious evening meal.

47

Yakitori

Serves 4

Most people have heard of *yakitori*. It is chicken kebabs, popular as a snack-like dish, and particularly good eaten with a glass of beer!

3 whole chicken breasts
14 oz (400 g) chicken livers
3 or 4 leeks (only the white part)
2 fl oz (50 ml) salad oil
4 fl oz (100 ml) soy sauce
1½ tbsp sugar
1 clove garlic, mashed
1 tbsp grated ginger root
1½ tbsp sake (or dry sherry)
Red chilli pepper powder

Cut the chicken and liver into bite-sized pieces, and cut the leeks into ¾ inch (2 cm) pieces. Mix together the salad oil, soy sauce, sugar, garlic, ginger, and *sake* and marinate the chicken and liver in this mixture for 2 hours.

Preheat a grill. Alternate on skewers the chicken, leeks and livers. Grill for 5 minutes, turn and grill for 5 minutes more or until a few charred spots appear, basting with the soy sauce mixture.

When cooked, serve immediately sprinkled lightly with chilli pepper.

Artist unknown

Zōsui with Chicken

Zōsui is a little like Italian risotto, but with more
soup in the rice, and a more simple taste (but delicious!). Japanese folklore has it that when you
have a cold, generous helpings of *zōsui* will make
you feel better, warming you from the inside. You
can use leftover rice, so it is economical as well.

There are many types of *zōsui*. This one is made
with chicken. Use homemade chicken soup if possible, but chicken bouillon could be used.

6 cups of leftover rice
7 oz (200 g) chicken
1 leek, washed
2 eggs
2 tsp sugar
¼ tsp salt
Salad oil
2½ pints (1.1 litres) chicken soup
½ tbsp salt
4 fl oz (100 ml) sake

Put the rice in a bamboo basket (or strainer) and wash briefly
under hot water to take away the stickiness. Shake off excess
water. Cut the chicken into bite-sized pieces and the leeks
diagonally into ¾ inch (2 cm) pieces.

Mix the eggs, sugar and ¼ tsp of salt in a small bowl. Pour
some salad oil into a pan and cook the eggs to make a very

thin pancake. Cut it into ½ inch (1.5 cm) strips and set aside.

In a large pan, boil a mixture of the soup, ½ tbsp salt, *sake* and chicken. When the chicken is cooked add the rice and bring to the boil. Quickly add the egg strips and the leek and cook for 30 seconds. Don't overcook! Eat immediately.

How luxuriant the young foliage
Leaving only Mount Fuji unburied
Buson [1715–1783]

Oyako Donburi

Donburi means 'bowl which is made of thick earthenware', and so 'something' *donburi* is a rice meal with a specific food on hot rice in a bowl. There are several kinds of famous *donburi*, but this *oyako donburi* is the most popular, with a chicken and egg mixture topping.

Prepare a mixture of:
3 fl oz (75 ml) *dashi*
1 tbsp soy sauce
1 tbsp *mirin*
1 tbsp *sake*
2 teaspoons sugar

3 oz (80 g) chicken breast

½ small onion, thinly sliced

2 *shiitake* (or mushrooms) cut in half

Cress

1 egg, lightly beaten

Hot rice, to serve

In a small pan bring the *dashi* mixture to the boil. Add the chicken, onion and *shiitake* to the mixture and turn down the heat to medium. When the chicken is cooked, sprinkle the cress and pour the stirred egg on it. When the egg is half-cooked, cover the pan with a lid and turn off the heat. Allow the pan to stand for a few minutes and then about three-quarters fill a *donburi* with hot rice, and put the chicken mixture on it. Serve immediately.

ゑど　黒戸へ小松内門
倍み侍ぶ色移んて
昔ぶ人におぐ

まして時侍さか

せさゆきまぴいしと

忘れ侍ぶ雀に

みろ侍本り
をきを
ゑど　黒戸と
つ
ゑぞ

Nishikawa Sukenobu

Chūka Donburi

Another famous *donburi* dish, *chūka* means 'Chinese'. Japanese people love Chinese food and frequently adapt it for an everyday meal as popular as Japanese cuisine. This is a recipe of Chinese origin which, unlike some, does not include ingredients which are hard to get or are quite complicated to prepare.

For this dish, the mixture of pork, chicken, bamboo shoots is served on hot rice.

2 oz (50 g) pork
2 oz (50 g) chicken
2 tsp soy sauce
2 tsp *sake*
1 tbsp salad oil
1 shrimp
2 oz (50 g) bamboo shoots, thinly sliced
2 *shiitake*, sliced
1 oz (30g) boiled snow peas
½ tbsp soy sauce
2 fl oz (50 ml) soup
¾ tbsp sugar
1 tsp ginger juice
Salt and pepper

54

½ tbsp water	
1 tsp corn starch	
Sesame oil	
Hot rice, to serve	

日
本
の
料
理

Cut the pork and chicken into bite-sized pieces and coat with the soy sauce and *sake* and leave for a while.

Using a wok, heat the salad oil over a high heat and cook the pork and chicken. Add the shrimp, bamboo shoots, *shiitake* and snow peas and cook for a few minutes more.

In a small pot, mix the soy sauce, soup, sugar and ginger juice and season with salt and pepper. Heat up and add a mixture of the water and corn starch and bring to a low boil.

Add the meat and vegetables mixture to this and heat up again. Add a few drops of sesame oil. Half fill *donburi* with hot rice and put the mixture on top of it. Serve immediately.

What joy it was, sandals in hand,
To wade across the summer stream!
Buson [1715–1783]

Chinese-style Deep-fried Chicken

This tasty deep-fried chicken with the taste of soy sauce and ginger is good for an evening dinner but also for an afternoon picnic. It is quite tasty cold.

4 chicken thighs with bones
4 drumsticks
2 tsp ginger juice
2 tbsp *sake*
3~4 tbsp soy sauce
2 tbsp flour
3 tbsp corn starch
Salad oil

Wash the chicken pieces and then dry completely using a paper towel. In a shallow casserole dish, mix the ginger juice, *sake* and soy sauce. Marinate the chicken in this for 1 hour turning occasionally.

Mix together the flour and corn starch and sprinkle the mixture over the chicken. Mix with the sauce by hand.

In a deep pan heat the salad oil to 170°C, put in half of the chicken and reduce the heat to medium. Deep fry the chicken until the bones come out. Remove and deep fry the rest.

Just before serving, heat up the oil to 180 °C and deep fry the chicken again for another 30 seconds. This will make it more crisp and tasty.

Fish Patties

This is like hamburgers made with tuna instead of minced beef. You could make these patties smaller than beef hamburgers.

14 oz (400 g) canned tuna, minced
1 egg, beaten
1 oz (25 g) bread crumbs
2 tbsp *mirin*
1 tbsp ginger juice
2 tbsp soy sauce
2 tbsp flour
4 oz (100 ml) salad oil
Topping: Soy sauce and tomato ketcup, or chilli sauce

Mix well the tuna, egg, breadcrumbs *mirin*, ginger juice and soy sauce. Form small hamburger-sized patties and coat in flour.

Heat a frying pan and add the oil. When it is hot, fry the fish patties on both sides until well browned.

If you wish, make a sauce of soy sauce and ketchup or use chilli sauce as a topping.

Oh! I enjoyed the evening cool
With one who doesn't speak all he thinks
Hyakuchi [1748–1836]

Artist unknown

水道橋
の不
二

Hokusai

Sunomono with Shrimps

Serves 4

This is not a main meal, just a side dish. *Sunomono* means 'vinegared things' (*su* means vinegar). This is a mixture of cucumber with shrimps with the taste of vinegar.

½ cucumber, thinly sliced
6 tbsp vinegar
2 tbsp soy sauce
1 tsp salt
2 tbsp sugar
8 oz (250 g) boiled shrimps, kept warm

Sprinkle the sliced cucumber with salt and leave for 5 minutes. Squeeze out the excess water using your hands, rinse off the salt and drain.

Mix the vinegar, soy sauce, salt and sugar together and add the shrimps and cucumbers. Serve at once while the shrimps are still warm.

Bright is the moon! If ever reborn
May I be a pine on a mountain peak!
Ryōta [1707–1787]

Rolled Pork with Vegetables

Serves 4

This is not a particularly Japanese meal, but rather a Japanese taste because of the soy sauce and *sake*.

6 *shiitake* (or mushrooms)
3 oz (75 g) green beans
8 very thin slices of pork loin
1½ tbsp salad oil
3 tbsp sugar
4 tbsp soy sauce
1½ tbsp *sake*

Cut the *shiitake* into thin pieces. Boil the beans in salted water for 5~6 minutes.

On four of the pork slices, roll up one-quarter of the *shiitake* for each and hold with a toothpick or cocktail stick. On the remaining four slices, roll a quarter of the beans for each and secure with a toothpick or cocktail stick.

Heat up the salad oil in a pan and fry the rolled pork, turning over on a medium heat. When they are a little charred, add the sugar, soy sauce and *sake*. Cook for a further 2~3 minutes and then remove from the pan. Reduce the leftover liquid by boiling for a few minutes.

Cut each slice into two pieces, place on a warmed serving plate and pour the sauce over them. Serve while hot.

Oh, snail, climb Mount Fuji,
Very, very slowly
Issa [1763–1827]

Chicken Sashimi

Serves 4

Most people have heard of *sashimi*, the famous Japanese sliced raw fish eaten with soy sauce and small amounts of *wasabi* (which is a very hot, green horse radish).

In this recipe chicken is used instead of fish and it's not raw!

3 boneless chicken thighs
Salt
1 leek (2 inch (5 cm) of the green part)
4~5 thin slices of ginger
1½ tbsp *sake*
Wasabi
Soy sauce or lemon juice

Prick the skin of the chicken with a fork and sprinkle salt on both sides.

Put the leek and ginger in a deep ovenproof, dish. Place the chicken on top and sprinkle with *sake*.

Place the dish with the chicken in a boiling steamer and steam over a high heat for 20 minutes.

Remove the chicken to a plate and sprinkle with the remaining liquid after removing the leek and ginger. When cool, put them in the refrigerator, turning them over occasionally.

Cut the chicken into thin slices.

In a small bowl mix a little *wasabi* with soy sauce or lemon juice. Dip the chicken in this and eat.

Katsukawa Shunchō

Hokusai